LIFE'S LITTLE BOOK OF
WISDOM FOR
MEN

© 2008 by Barbour Publishing, Inc.

ISBN 978-1-59789-956-7

All rights reserved. No part of this publication may be reproduced or transmitted for commercial purposes, except for brief quotations in printed reviews, without written permission of the publisher.

Scripture quotations marked KJV are taken from the King James Version of the Bible.

Scripture quotations marked NIV are taken from the HOLY BIBLE, NEW INTERNATIONAL VERSION®. NIV®. Copyright © 1973, 1978, 1984 by International Bible Society. Used by permission of Zondervan. All rights reserved.

Scripture quotations marked NLT are taken from the *Holy Bible,* New Living Translation, copyright © 1996. Used by permission of Tyndale House Publishers, Inc. Wheaton, Illinois 60189, U.S.A. All rights reserved.

Scripture quotations marked NRSV are taken from the New Revised Standard Version Bible, copyright 1989, Division of Christian Education of the National Council of the Churches of Christ in the United States of America. Used by permission. All rights reserved.

Cover image © Ryuichi Sato

Published by Barbour Publishing, Inc., P.O. Box 719, Uhrichsville, Ohio 44683, www.barbourbooks.com

Our mission is to publish and distribute inspirational products offering exceptional value and biblical encouragement to the masses.

Printed in China.

LIFE'S LITTLE BOOK OF WISDOM FOR
MEN

BARBOUR

The secret of happiness
is not in doing what one likes
but in liking what one has to do.

J. M. BARRIE

Where is the wise man? Where is the scholar? Where is the philosopher of this age? Has not God made foolish the wisdom of the world? For since in the wisdom of God the world through its wisdom did not know him, God was pleased through the foolishness of what was preached to save those who believe.

1 CORINTHIANS 1:20-21 NIV

Be content with your surroundings
but not with yourself till you
have made the most of them.

UNKNOWN

It is unwise to be too sure of one's own wisdom. It is healthy to be reminded that the strongest might weaken and the wisest might err.

MAHATMA GANDHI

God asks no one whether he will accept life. That is not the choice. You must take it. The only choice is how.

Henry Ward Beecher

But the meek shall inherit the earth;
and shall delight themselves
in the adundance of peace.

PSALM 37:11 KJV

We find in life exactly what we put into it.

RALPH WALDO EMERSON

The greatest use of life is to spend it for something that will outlast it.

WILLIAM JAMES

Time wasted is existence;
time used is life.

EDWARD YOUNG

There never was any heart truly great and generous, that was not also tender and compassionate.

ROBERT SOUTH

Seek the LORD your God,
you will find him if you look
for him with all your heart
and with all your soul.

DEUTERONOMY 4:29 NIV

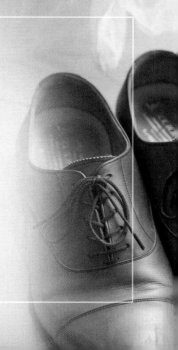

Peace is not something you wish for;
it's something you make,
something you do, something you are,
and something you give away.

ROBERT FULGHUM

Do not let trifles disturb your tranquility of mind. . . .
Life is too precious to be sacrificed for the nonessential and transient. . . .
Ignore the inconsequential.

GRENVILLE KLEISER

One falsehood spoils a thousand truths.

AFRICAN PROVERB

If you ever find happiness by hunting it, you will find it as the old woman did her lost spectacles, safe on her own nose the whole time.

JOSH BILLINGS

Command those who are rich in this present world not to be arrogant nor to put their hope in wealth, which is so uncertain, but to put their hope in God, who richly provides us with everything for our enjoyment.

1 TIMOTHY 6:17 NIV

All that is essential for
the triumph of evil is that
good men do nothing.

EDMUND BURKE

One word frees us of all the weight and pain of life: That word is love.

SOPHOCLES

Time is the coin of your life.
It is the only coin you have,
and only you can determine how
it will be spent. Be careful lest you
let other people spend it for you.

CARL SANDBURG

No one can excel in everything.
The decades demand decisions.
Choose wisely. Your choices pinpoint
your priorities and determine your destiny.
Use it or lose it.

PATRICIA SOUDER

He said to his disciples, "Therefore I tell you, do not worry about your life, what you will eat, or about your body, what you will wear. For life is more than food, and the body more than clothing. Consider the ravens: they neither sow nor reap, they have neither storehouse nor barn, and yet God feeds them. Of how much more value are you than the birds!"

LUKE 12:22-24 NRSV

I find the great thing in this world
is not so much where we stand as
in what direction we are moving.

Oliver Wendell Holmes

Happiness is like perfume; you can't pour it on someone else without getting a few drops on yourself.

JAMES VAN DER ZEE

The well of Providence is deep.
It's the buckets we bring to it that are small.

MARY WEBB

Wisdom is knowing what to do next. Skill is knowing how to do it. Virtue is doing it.

THOMAS JEFFERSON

Give instruction to a wise man,
and he will be yet wiser: teach a just man,
and he will increase in learning.

PROVERBS 9:9 KJV

*Let him who would move
the world first move himself.*

SENECA

The real joy of life is in its play.
Play is anything we do for the joy and
love of doing it, apart from any profit,
compulsion, or sense of duty.
It is the real living of life.

WALTER RAUSCHENBUSCH

Don't rob yourself the joy of this season by wishing you were in a future or a past one.

CHERYL BIEHL

There are better things ahead
than any we leave behind.

C. S. LEWIS

So I tell you, whatever you ask for in prayer, believe that you have received it, and it will be yours.

MARK 11:24 NRSV

Don't put off for tomorrow what you can do today, because if you enjoy it today, you can do it again tomorrow.

JAMES A. MICHENER

Fill up the crevices of time with the things that matter most.

AMY CARMICHAEL

Experience is the mother of truth;
and by experience we learn wisdom.

WILLIAM SHIPPEN JR.

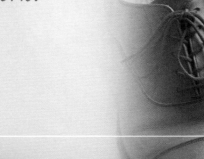

The beginning is the most important part of the work.

PLATO

For surely I know the plans I have
for you, says the Lord, plans for your
welfare and not for harm,
to give you a future with hope.

JEREMIAH **29:11** NRSV

I am only one, but I am still one;
I cannot do everything, but I can
still do something; and because I
cannot do everything I will not refuse
to do the something that I can do.

EDWARD EVERETT HALE

*No matter how far you have gone
on the wrong road, turn back.*

TURKISH PROVERB

The important thing is this:
To be able at any moment to
sacrifice what we are for
what we could become.

CHARLES DU BOIS

Maturity begins to grow when you can sense your concern for others outweighing your concern for yourself.

JOHN MACNAUGHTON

Now faith is being sure of what we hope for and certain of what we do not see. . . . By faith we understand that the universe was formed at God's command, so that what is seen was not made out of what was visible.

HEBREWS 11:1, 3 NIV

It is the greatest of all mistakes to do nothing because you can only do a little. Do what you can.

SYDNEY SMITH

Practice as if you are the worst,
perform as if you are the best.

ANONYMOUS

God loves each one of us as if there were only one of us.

AUGUSTINE

Everything that is done in
the world is done by hope.

MARTIN LUTHER

Trust in the LORD with all your heart and lean not on your own understanding; in all your ways acknowledge him, and he will make your paths straight.

PROVERBS 3:5-6 NIV

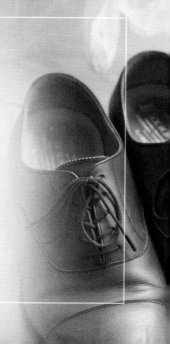

Life is either a daring adventure or nothing.

HELEN KELLER

The way a team plays as a whole determines its success. You may have the greatest bunch of individual stars in the world, but if they don't play together, the club won't be worth a dime.

BABE RUTH

I thank Thee, O LORD, that thou hast so set eternity within my heart that no earthly thing can ever satisfy me wholly.

JOHN BAILLIE

The poor man is not he who is without a cent but he who is without a dream.

HARRY KEMP

The moon marks off the seasons, and the sun knows when to go down. . . . Then man goes out to his work, to his labor until evening. How many are your works, O LORD! In wisdom you made them all.

PSALM 104:19, 23-24 NIV

A good hockey player plays where the puck is. A great hockey player plays where the puck is going to be.

WAYNE GRETZKY

Attempt great things for God;
expect great things from God.

WILLIAM CAREY

There is nothing like a dream
to create the future.

Courage is the power of being mastered by and possessed with an idea.

Phillips Brooks

We know that in all things God works for the good of those who love him, who have been called according to his purpose.

ROMANS 8:28 NIV

No man who is occupied in
doing a very difficult thing,
and doing it very well,
ever loses his self-respect.

GEORGE BERNARD SHAW

It doesn't matter who scores
the points, it's who can get
the ball to the scorer.

LARRY BIRD

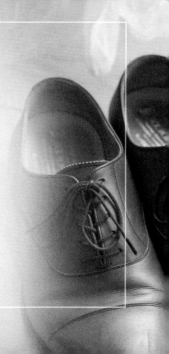

God is with us,
and His power is around us.

CHARLES H. SPURGEON

Worry is interest paid on trouble before it falls due.

W. R. INGE

Wise words bring many benefits,
and hard work brings rewards.

PROVERBS 12:14 NLT

Be nice to people on your way up
because you'll meet them
on your way down.

WILSON MIZNER

Start by doing what's necessary,
then what's possible, and suddenly
you are doing the impossible.

FRANCIS OF ASSISI

The celestial order and beauty of the universe compel me to admit that there is some excellent and eternal Being who deserves the respect and homage of men.

CICERO

If we had no winter, the spring would not be so pleasant: if we did not sometimes taste of adversity, prosperity would not be so welcome.

ANNE BRADSTREET

We can rejoice, too, when we run
into problems and trials, for we know
that they help us develop endurance.
And endurance develops strength of
character, and character strengthens
our confident hope of salvation.

ROMANS 5:3-4 NLT

Character is what you are in the dark.

Dwight L. Moody

Always be in a state of expectancy,
and see that you leave room for
God to come in as He likes.

Oswald Chambers

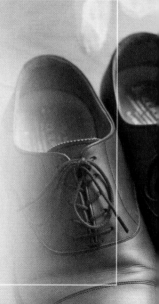

A candle loses nothing of its light
by lighting another candle.

Unknown

When written in Chinese the word "crisis" is composed of two characters. One represents danger and the other represents opportunity.

JOHN F. KENNEDY

*In returning and rest shall
ye be saved; in quietness and in
confidence shall be your strength.*

Isaiah 30:15 KJV

Experience is not what happens to a man.
It is what a man does with
what happens to him.

ALDOUS HUXLEY

We were not sent into this world
to do anything into which we
cannot put our hearts.

JOHN RUSKIN

Let nothing disturb you, let nothing frighten you: everything passes away except God; God alone is sufficient.

TERESA OF AVILA

I cannot give you the formula for success, but I can give you the formula for failure—which is: Try to please everybody.

HERBERT B. SWOPE

There is a time for everything, and a season for every activity under heaven.

ECCLESIASTES 3:1 NIV

When I was a boy of fourteen, my father was so ignorant I could hardly stand to have the old man around. But when I got to be twenty-one, I was astonished at how much he had learned in seven years.

MARK TWAIN

The voyage of discovery is not in seeking new landscapes but in having new eyes.

MARCEL PROUST

Learn from the mistakes of others, for you don't have enough time to make them all yourself!

MARCUS AURELIUS

*The really great man is the man
who makes every man feel great.*

G. K. CHESTERTON

Then Christ will make his home
in your hearts as you trust in him.
Your roots will grow down into
God's love and keep you strong.
And may you have the power to
understand, as all God's people should,
how wide, how long, how high,
and how deep his love is.

EPHESIANS 3:17-18 NLT

*self-confidence is the first requisite
to great undertakings.*

SAMUEL JOHNSON

Nothing is so strong as
gentleness, and nothing
so gentle as real strength.

FRANCIS DE SALES

Our Lord has written the promise of the resurrection, not in books alone, but in every leaf in springtime.

MARTIN LUTHER

Great beauty, great strength,
and great riches are really and truly of
no great use; a right heart exceeds all.

BENJAMIN FRANKLIN

Guard your heart above all else,
for it determines the course of your life.

PROVERBS 4:23 NLT

Happiness will never come to those
who fail to appreciate what
they already have.

UNKNOWN

There is a past which is gone forever,
but there is a future which is still our own.

F. W. ROBERTSON

This is the miracle that happens
every time to those who really
love; the more they give,
the more they possess.

RAINER MARIA RILKE

There is no limit to what can be accomplished if it doesn't matter who gets the credit.

RALPH WALDO EMERSON

Give all your worries and cares to
God, for he cares about you.

1 PETER 5:7 NLT

We make a living by what we get;
we make a life by what we give.

SIR WINSTON CHURCHILL

Give thanks for the unknown
blessings already on their way.

NATIVE AMERICAN PROVERB

Be great in little things.

FRANCIS XAVIER

Whatever you are, be a good one.

ABRAHAM LINCOLN

And now these three remain:
faith, hope, and love.
But the greatest of these is love.

1 CORINTHIANS 13:13 NIV

You can't build a reputation on what you are going to do.

HENRY FORD

We are made to reach beyond our grasp.

OSWALD CHAMBERS

The aim, if reached or not,
makes great the life.

ROBERT BROWNING

Pray to God, but keep rowing to shore.

RUSSIAN PROVERB

Listen to advice and accept instruction, and in the end you will be wise.

PROVERBS 19:20 NIV

*It is easier to do a job right
than to explain why you didn't.*

MARTIN VAN BUREN

The reason for loving God is God Himself, and the measure in which we should love Him is to love Him without measure.

BERNARD OF CLAIRVAUX

The sun. . .in its full glory, either at rising or setting—this, and many other like blessings we enjoy daily; and for the most of them, because they are so common, most men forget to pay their praises. But let not us.

IZAAK WALTON

Stand up to your obstacles and do something about them. You will find that they haven't half the strength you think they have.

Norman Vincent Peale

My son, do not despise the LORD's
discipline and do not resent his rebuke,
because the LORD disciplines those he
loves, as a father the son he delights in.

PROVERBS 3:11-12 NIV

Joy comes from using your potential.

WILL SCHULTZ

My great concern is not whether God is on our side; my great concern is to be on God's side.

ABRAHAM LINCOLN

*Truth is the beginning of
every good thing,
both in heaven and on earth.*

UNKNOWN

A pessimist sees the difficulty in every opportunity; an optimist sees the opportunity in every difficulty.

SIR WINSTON CHURCHILL

For our light affliction, which is but for a moment, worketh for us a far more exceeding and eternal weight of glory.

2 CORINTHIANS 4:17 KJV

Well done is better than well said.

BENJAMIN FRANKLIN

Keep your face to the sunshine
and you cannot see the shadow.

HELEN KELLER

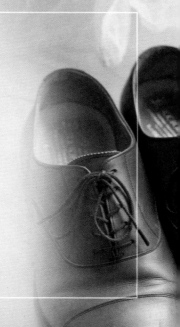

*Let us not hurry so in our pace of living
that we lose sight of the art of living.*

SIR FRANCIS BACON

Everyone has a unique role
to fill in the world and
is important in some respect.
Everyone, including and perhaps
especially you, is indispensable.

NATHANIEL HAWTHORNE

When a man's ways are pleasing to the LORD, he makes even his enemies live at peace with him.

PROVERBS 16:7 NIV

Do what you can, with what you have, where you are.

THEODORE ROOSEVELT

*Do not go where the path may lead,
go instead where there is no path
and leave a trail.*

RALPH WALDO EMERSON

Faith is to believe what we do not see; and the reward of this faith is to see what we believe.

AUGUSTINE

A gentle word, a kind look,
a good-natured smile can work
wonders and accomplish miracles.

WILLIAM HAZLITT

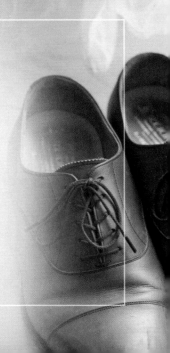

"The joy of the LORD is your strength!"

NEHEMIAH 8:10 NLT

Any intelligent fool can make things bigger, more complex, and more violent. It takes a touch of genius—and a lot of courage—to move in the opposite direction.

ALBERT EINSTEIN

The ordinary acts we practice
every day at home are of more
importance to the soul than
their simplicity might suggest.

THOMAS MORE

*Greed is a fat demon with a small mouth,
and whatever you feed it is never enough.*

JANWILLEM VAN DE WETERING

Right is right, even if everyone
is against it; and wrong is wrong,
even if everyone is for it.

WILLIAM PENN

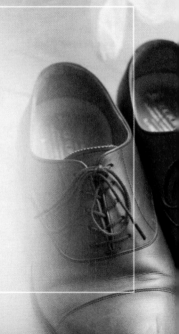

Clothe yourselves with love, which binds everything together in perfect harmony.

COLOSSIANS 3:14 NRSV

Associate yourself with men of good quality if you esteem your own reputation; for it is better to be alone than in bad company.

GEORGE WASHINGTON

He turns not back who is bound to a star.

LEONARDO DA VINCI

The smallest bit of obedience opens heaven, and the deepest truths of God immediately become ours.

OSWALD CHAMBERS

*You may be disappointed if you fail,
but you are doomed if you don't try.*

BEVERLY SILLS

Those who hope in the LORD
will renew their strength.
They will soar on wings like eagles;
they will run and not grow weary,
they will walk and not be faint.

ISAIAH 40:31 NIV

Life is what we make it.
Always has been, always will be.

GRANDMA MOSES

The creation of a thousand
forests is in one acorn.

RALPH WALDO EMERSON

The riches that are in the heart cannot be stolen.

RUSSIAN PROVERB

Shoot for the moon.
Even if you miss,
you'll land among the stars.

LES BROWN

Do you not know? Have you not heard? The LORD is the everlasting God, the Creator of the ends of the earth. He will not grow tired or weary, and his understanding no one can fathom. He gives strength to the weary and increases the power of the weak.

ISAIAH 40:28-29 NIV

'Tis a lesson you should heed:
Try, try, try again.
If at first you don't succeed,
try, try, try again.

W. E. HICKSON

Make no little plans; they have no magic to stir men's blood and probably themselves will not be realized. Make big plans; aim high in hope and work.

DANIEL H. BURNHAM

The thought of You stirs us so deeply
that we cannot be content unless
we praise You, because You have
made us for Yourself and our hearts
find no peace until they rest in You.

AUGUSTINE

Great works are performed not by
strength but by perseverance.

SAMUEL JOHNSON

Blessed is the nation whose God is the LORD.

PSALM 33:12 NIV

What lies behind us and what lies before us are tiny matters compared to what lies within us.

RALPH WALDO EMERSON

*Think. . .of the world
you carry within you.*

RAINER MARIA RILKE

Pleasure is very seldom found where it is sought. Our brightest blazes are commonly kindled by unexpected sparks.

SAMUEL JOHNSON

Look at a day when you are supremely satisfied at the end. It is not a day when you lounge around doing nothing; it is when you have had everything to do, and you have done it.

MARGARET THATCHER

Come close to God,
and God will come close to you.

JAMES 4:8 NLT

When one door closes, another one opens, but we often look so long and regretfully at the closed door that we fail to see the one that has opened for us.

ALEXANDER GRAHAM BELL

Time, indeed, is a sacred gift,
and each day is a little life.

SIR JOHN LUBBOCK

I would rather walk with God in
the dark than go alone in the light.

Mary Gardiner Brainard

*Look at life through the windshield,
not the rearview mirror.*

BYRD BAGGETT

God is our refuge and strength,
a very present help in trouble.
Therefore will not we fear,
though the earth be removed,
and though the mountains be
carried into the midst of the sea.

PSALM 46:1-2 KJV

Every person you meet knows something you don't. Learn from them.

H. JACKSON BROWN

God writes the gospel not in the Bible alone, but on trees and flowers and clouds and stars.

MARTIN LUTHER

There is nothing but God's grace.
We walk upon it; we breathe it; we live
and die by it; it makes the nails and
the axles of the universe.

ROBERT LOUIS STEVENSON

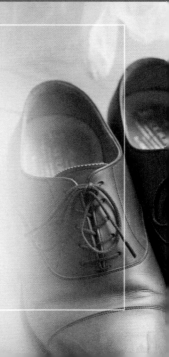

The important thing is
not to stop questioning.

ALBERT EINSTEIN

For I command you today to love the LORD
your God, to walk in his ways, and to
keep his commands, decrees, and laws;
then you will live and increase,
and the LORD your God will bless you.

DEUTERONOMY 30:16 NIV

If Columbus had turned back,
no one would have blamed him.
Of course, no one would have
remembered him either.

UNKNOWN

Our Creator would never have made
such lovely days, and have given
us the deep hearts to enjoy them,
above and beyond all thought,
unless we were meant to be immortal.

NATHANIEL HAWTHORNE

True silence is the rest of
the mind; it is to the spirit
what sleep is to the body,
nourishment and refreshment.

WILLIAM PENN

Life is like a baseball game. You do not have to succeed seven out of ten times, and you can still make the all-star team.

ANONYMOUS

God's peace. . .exceeds anything
we can understand. His peace will
guard your hearts and minds
as you live in Christ Jesus.

PHILIPPIANS 4:7 NLT

Choose a job you love, and you will never have to work a day in your life.

Confucius

All truths are easy to understand
once they are discovered;
the point is to discover them.

GALILEO

God's fingers can touch nothing
but to mold it into loveliness.

GEORGE MACDONALD

They can conquer who believe they can.

RALPH WALDO EMERSON

He has showed you, O man, what is good.
And what does the LORD require of you?
To act justly and to love mercy and
to walk humbly with your God.

MICAH 6:8 NIV

Knowledge is proud that it knows so much; wisdom is humble that it knows no more.

WILLIAM COWPER

To me, every hour of the day and night
is an unspeakably perfect miracle.

WALT WHITMAN

Your only treasures are those which you carry in your heart.

DEMOPHILUS

Vision without action is a daydream.
Action without vision is a nightmare.

JAPANESE PROVERB

Don't turn your back on wisdom, for she will protect you. Love her, and she will guard you. Getting wisdom is the wisest thing you can do! And whatever else you do, develop good judgment.

PROVERBS 4:6-7 NLT

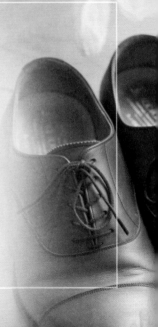

"But" is a fence over which few leap.

GERMAN PROVERB

If we learn how to give of ourselves, to forgive others, and to live with thanksgiving, we need not seek happiness. It will seek us.

UNKNOWN

*What the heart has once owned
and had, it shall never lose.*

HENRY WARD BEECHER

Do not wait for extraordinary
situations to do good;
try to use ordinary situations.

JEAN PAUL RICHTER

Commit your work to the Lord,
and your plans will be established.

PROVERBS 16:3 NRSV

A loving person lives in a loving world. A hostile person lives in a hostile world; everyone you meet is your mirror.

KEN KEYES JR.

It isn't the great big pleasures
that count the most; it's making a
great deal out of the little ones.

JEAN WEBSTER

When the soul has laid down
its faults at the feet of God,
it feels as though it had wings.

EUGÉNIE DE GUÉRIN

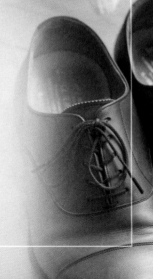

Understanding is knowing what to do;
wisdom is knowing what to do next;
virtue is actually doing it.

TRISTAN GYLBERD

The heavens declare the glory
of God; the skies proclaim
the work of his hands.

PSALM 19:1 NIV

Remember that happiness is a way of travel—not a destination.

Roy M. Goodman

The glory is not in never failing,
but in rising every time you fail.

CHINESE PROVERB

God gives us always strength enough, and sense enough, for everything He wants us to do.

JOHN RUSKIN

Every experience God gives us, every person He puts in our lives, is the perfect preparation for the future that only He can see.

Corrie ten Boom

Cast thy burden upon the LORD,
and he shall sustain thee: he shall
never suffer the righteous to be moved.

PSALM 55:22 KJV

You can't do anything about the length of your life, but you can do something about its width and depth.

EVAN ESAR